What's left ?

What's left ?

Written and illustrated by Judi Barrett

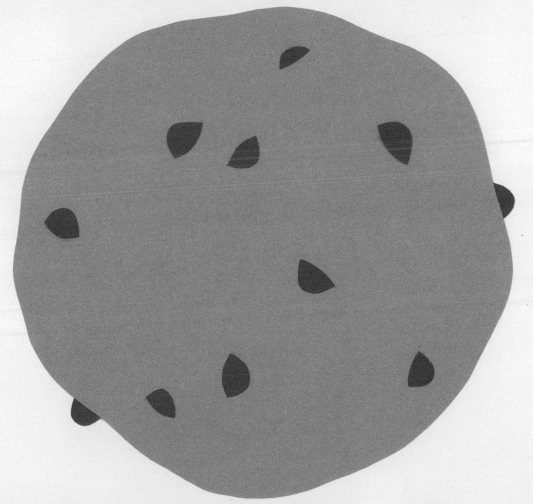

Atheneum   New York   1983

Library of Congress Cataloging in Publication Data

Barrett, Judi.
  What's left?

  SUMMARY: Answers such questions as "What's left after
you finish crying?" and "What's left after it rains?"
  [1. Questions and answers] I. Title
PZ7.B2752Wh [E] 81-12824
ISBN 0-689-30874-4   AACR2

Published simultaneously in Canada by
McClelland & Stewart, Ltd.
Manufactured by South China Printing Co., Hong Kong
First American Edition

What's left
after you've eaten your chocolate chip cookie?

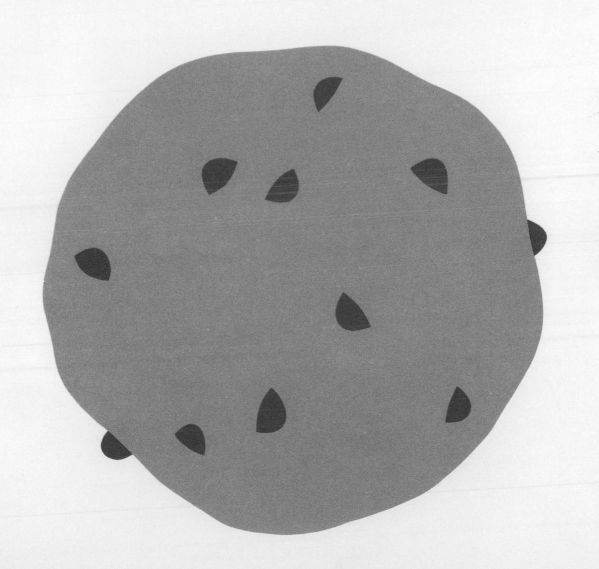

Cookie crumbs.

What's left
after it rains?

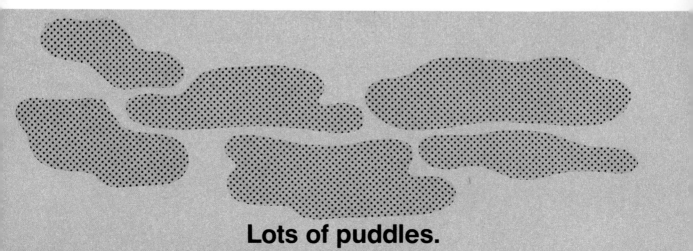

Lots of puddles.

What's left
after you finish crying?

A few tears.

What's left
after you've taken your bath?

A ring around the tub.

What's left
after you get out of bed in the morning?

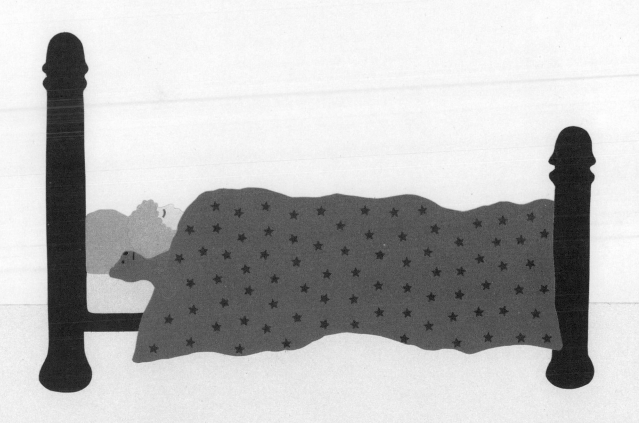

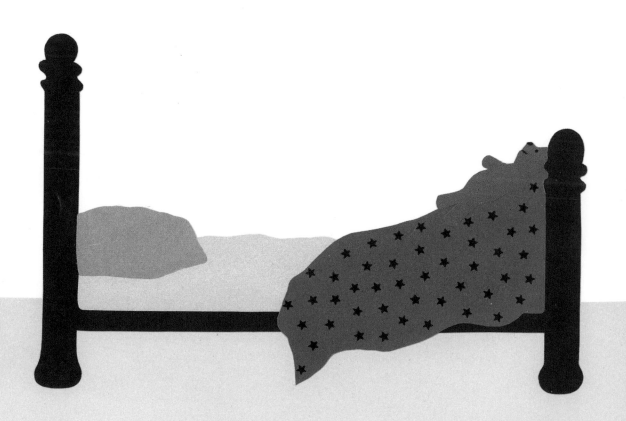

A warm spot.

What's left
after you've licked up all of your lollipop?

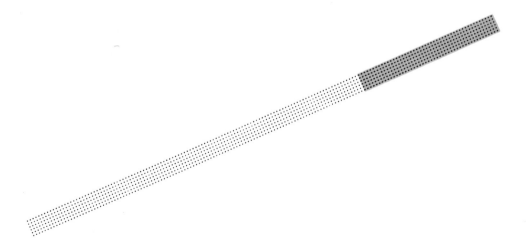

The stick.

What's left
after you bump into something hard?

A black and blue mark.

**What's left
after your birthday party is over?**

Presents.

What's left
after you drink all of your milk?

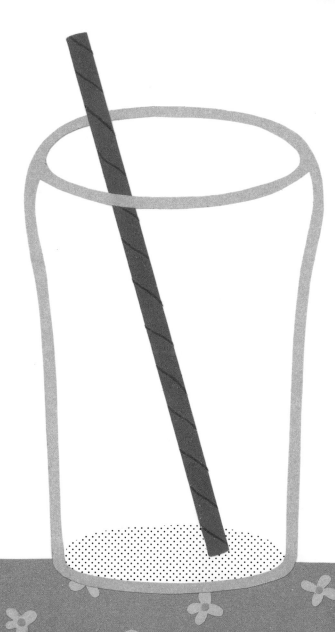

An empty glass.

What's left
after you turn off the television?

Silence.

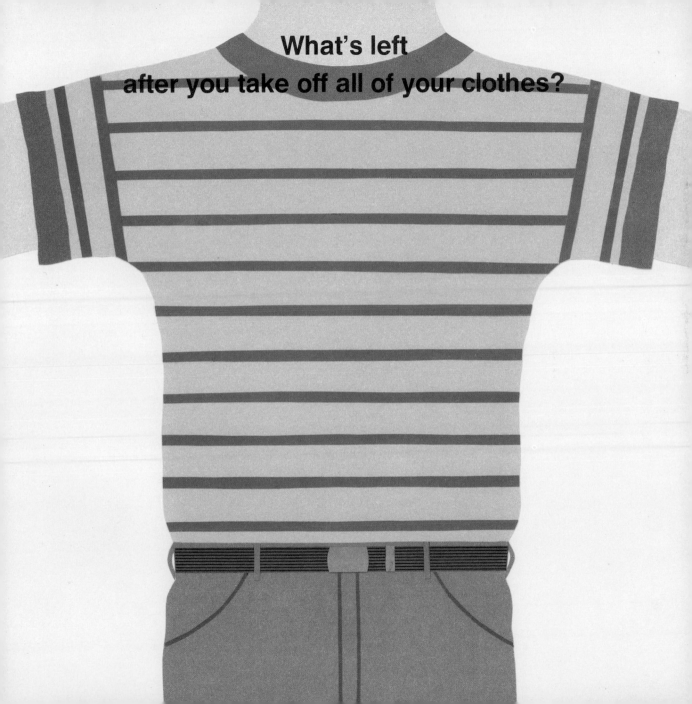

**What's left
after you take off all of your clothes?**

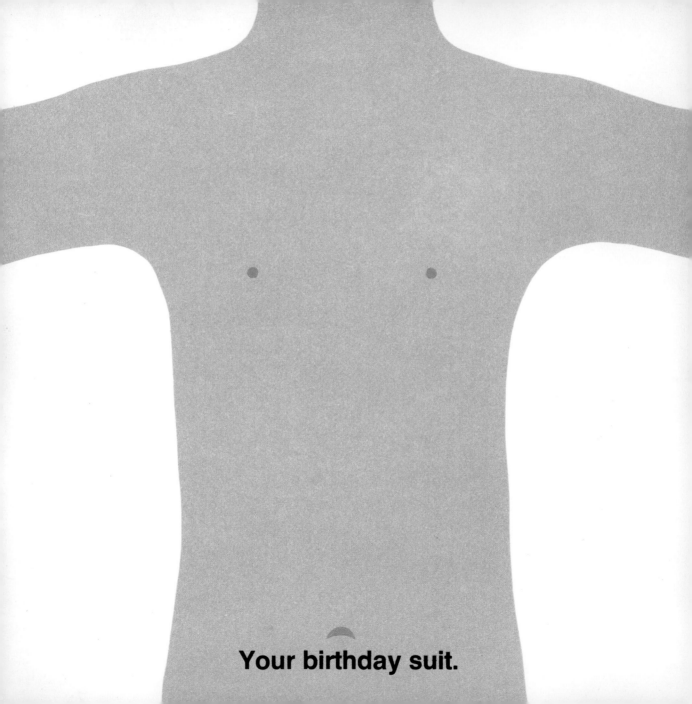
Your birthday suit.

What's left
after you've eaten too much candy?

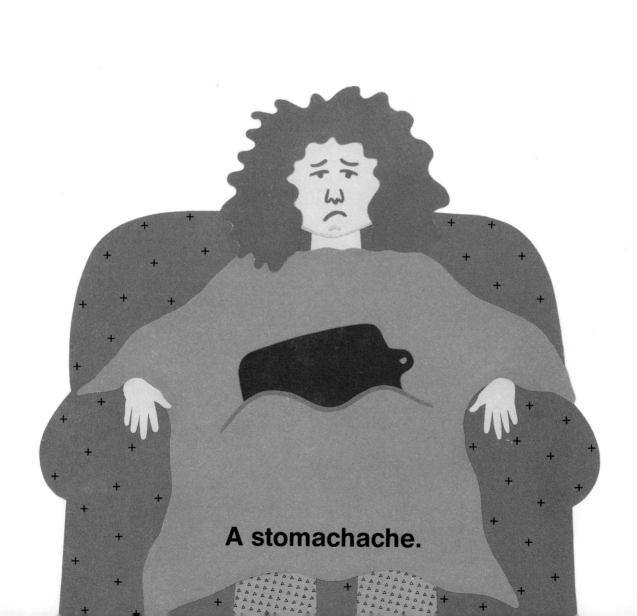

A stomachache.

What's left
after you go to sleep at night?

Your dreams.

**And what's left
after someone kisses you?**

A nice feeling.